Model Lessons for Literacy Instruction

Virtual Classroom Experiences

R. Carl Harris

PEARSON

Merrill
Prentice Hall

Upper Saddle River, New Jersey 07458
Columbus, Ohio 43235

Acquisitions Editor: Linda Ashe Montgomery
Developmental Editor: Hope Madden
Media Editor: Dan Parker
Editorial Assistant: Laura Weaver
Manufacturing Manager: Pamela D. Bennett

ISBN 0-13-112192-8
10 9 8 7 6 5 4 3 2 1

Contents

Introduction

Intimate familiarity with the practice of teaching is absolutely essential to effective teacher development. Simply reading and researching is not enough. But witnessing meaningful teaching first hand, observing master teachers, and reflecting on the actions, decisions, and artistry behind good teaching can bring you further along on your journey toward becoming a better teacher yourself.

But here we encounter a dilemma. Your need to analyze, discuss, or perhaps even criticize the decisions and actions of real teachers and students during the course of field experiences is antithetical to the needs of the students and teachers themselves.

While practice in living classrooms is an integral part of teacher preparation, there needs to be another way to uncover the deep meaning in the layers of content, pedagogy, culture, and environment in real classrooms. There should be a way to stop the action, review it, hold it up for scrutiny, and look at the action from various points of view. And there is – through virtual classroom experiences.

Virtual Classroom Experiences

One proven way to stop the action and hold it up for examination is through our Virtual Classroom Experiences CD –ROM. With this CD you have immediate access to living classroom examples of teaching and learning in literacy instruction. The examples provide context and anchor thinking in the realities of authentic classrooms.

The CD contains video clips of four different classrooms, grouped by grade level and lesson topic, which illustrate the process of teaching reading and writing to students in kindergarten, second, and fourth grades. Each group of clips shows a classroom teacher working through the stages of a reading lesson, including phonemic awareness, guided reading, comprehension strategies, and writing workshop.

This CD allows you to see wholes and parts, hear and read a variety of stakeholder perspectives, manipulate and create your own grouping of virtual classroom experiences, and assess the depth of your comprehension of the rich instructional layers inherent in these dynamic lessons.

Getting Started

To make the most of your virtual classroom experience you'll need to understand all the options available to you on this CD. You can begin by simply examining the four different classrooms and watching each lesson. But to truly uncover the layers of teacher decision making, theoretical connections, and pedagogy, you'll want not only to look closely at specific pieces of footage, analyzing each clip as well as the stakeholder perspectives, but manipulate and rework the clips for the layered, discreet information each holds.

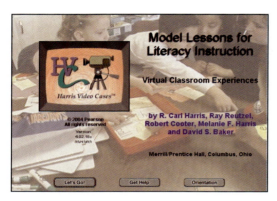

Begin your exploration by inserting the CD into your computer, and running the program with the "Click Me!" file. The CD will load, and you'll see the introductory screen. You'll be presented with three choices: Let's Go!, Get Help, and Orientation.

To start the case study, click the "Let's Go!" button. This will prompt you for a file. On your first use, click the "New File" button. The application will prompt you to save your file to your hard drive or a disk. Any work in the custom studies area will be saved to this file, so it's important that you complete this step when you first run the CD. Each time you run the CD again, it will again prompt you for a file. Use the file you originally created to resume previous work and add new custom studies, or begin a new file.

Using the Features of the CD

The chart on the following page illustrates the various features available on the CD. Please use this chart as a reference as you get acquainted with the CD's many functions.

The first clip in each of the lessons is titled "All Clips – Overview". This footage shows the entire video segment from beginning to end. The other eight segments break the full length footage into discreet teaching segments for your analysis.

Each topic includes 9 video clips. Individual clips are labeled according to the topics illustrated. Simply click on the thumbnail of one clip to watch the video segment. Across the bottom of the video screen you'll find buttons that allow you to pause, fast forward and rewind the clip.

As soon as a specific video clip is highlighted, comments concerning that segment also become available in the tabbed box below the video viewing window. You can choose from a lesson analysis from experts in the field, research literature on the subject, or thoughts from teachers and students alike. Listen to these stakeholders by clicking on the audio button.

ORIENTATION BUTTON
The Orientation feature provides a brief overview of the CD's content and organization. It will also alert you to the need and source of the QuickTime 6 software, the lack of which could cause technical problems when viewing footage.

You'll notice a Bonus Button on several clips. These buttons contain special additional content for specific segments, including lesson plans, and student artifacts.

STUDY BUTTONS
The video footage is divided into four different topics. You can choose from a kindergarten Phonemic Awareness lesson, a second grade Guided Reading lesson, Comprehension Strategies in a second grade classroom, and Writing Workshop in a fourth grade classroom.

CUSTOM STUDIES
The Custom Studies section allows you to customize your personal studies with your own comments, lesson plans, and quotes from the text of the CD. We will cover this in detail as well.

STUDY BUILDER
The Study Builder feature helps you to create your own study lesson using the video clips provided on the CD. We will discuss this in detail in a moment.

TEXT BUTTON
The text of the commentators for the CD is provided in this area, available for review, and ideal for copying and pasting to your own study.

NOTEPAD BUTTON
This feature allows you to take notes, copy and paste material from other sources, and save your ideas and insights. Each time you create something in the Notepad, you can save it individually to your hard drive or a disk, and then start a new file to jot down other ideas.

INTERNET BUTTON
Clicking on the Internet button launches an Internet browser allowing you to visit the links provided, or insert an Internet address and go to discussion groups, email, or other relevant sites that pertain to literacy.

HELP TOPICS
The "?" button in the lower left corner of the application window provides a wealth of clear, step by step information. Clicking on the ? button will open up the help file, where you will find explanations and directions for every button, and a guided tour through using the CD and building your own study.

Click on a topic in the Help Topics Menu to find a textual explanation of any item. Audio is provided as well, and will automatically play as the topic is discussed.

You'll notice a box marked "Autoplay" in the lower left corner while using the Help function. If that box is checked, the help topics will continuously play from one to the next. If you don't wish to use this feature, simply click the box to uncheck it. You can instead use the "Back" and "Next" buttons that accompany each piece of information to move from one to the next, or to go back and review something you've already seen.

From Theory to Practice

You will observe the practical applications of the educational theory you study with the classroom footage on this CD. When you look at the video clips for Phonemic Awareness in Kindergarten, for example, you'll see how well thought out literacy centers, like those you've studied, help create an effective literacy environment. Watch closely to see the way Ms. Clark helps her young learners recognize word families and phonemes, collaborate with each other, and use a simple learning center activity.

As you carefully observe each lesson, you will view many literacy processes put into practice and, unlike any field experience, you can watch them as many times as you'd like, reflecting on the decisions made and the strengths and weaknesses in each procedure.

You can compare instruction across the range of grades. How can small group instruction be effective in kindergarten, second, and fourth grades? As you observe instruction, you will become intimately familiar with four important components of teaching literacy: phonemic awareness, guided reading, comprehension, and writing. You'll learn the processes behind the planning of these lessons, see how they play out with students, acquaint yourself with the research and reasoning that goes into each lesson, and witness the successful literacy learning each produces.

As you review each classroom lesson, generate questions and answers to illustrate the layers of instruction you observe in each lesson. The following are some questions to consider.
- What elements of planning does each teacher use?
- What specific literacy concepts does each lesson cover?
- What makes each lesson effective for learning?
- How does the developmental level of each group of children dictate the way each teacher executes her lesson?

Creating Your Own Study

The Study Builder allows you to go significantly beyond the exploration of the studies already created. After all, there's a lot going on in each of these classrooms, and part of the power of having this footage is the ability to stop the action, review it, and consider distinct aspects of each lesson, or compare elements across the classrooms.

This CD allows you to think through your observations, assess and deepen your understandings of what you see, and share your conclusions by using the Study Builder to create your own studies.

Each custom study you create can be used to fulfill an assignment, or become part of your electronic teaching portfolio. Create as many custom studies as you like and examine your own understanding of any number of teaching strategies, techniques, and concerns.

Study Building

As you look at this footage you'll see much more than just a lesson on phonemic awareness or guided reading. You'll see classroom environments at work, ongoing assessment, classroom diversity. Teachers will work with struggling readers and writers. They'll manage their classrooms in small groups and in whole group instruction. The Study Builder feature gives you the opportunity to consider all these aspects of teaching and put together your own focused study.

For example, you know that the physical environment of the classroom will have an impact on your students and your teaching. What classroom environments work best for literacy study? What physical layout, what specific centers, what kind of space arrangement works for the teachers on the CD? As we walk you through the exciting Study Builder tool on your Virtual Classrooms CD ROM, these are the questions we will consider.

To create your own study, begin by clicking on the Study Builder button on the navigation bar.

To find the video data to support your focus, review various video segments in search of those most appropriate for your investigation. To do this, click on one of the 24 video clips at the bottom of the Study Builder Screen, then on the Play Video Button located above the 24 clips. As you consider specific clips, you can stop the play of each video either by clicking on the small X at

upper left corner of the video screen, or clicking on another video clip.

As you review the video clips you'll begin to see examples to support your own investigation. In our case, for instance, Clip 7—which is the Plan and Manage clip from Rhonda Blake's Second Grade Guided Reading lesson—helps us to look more closely at the physical environment of Rhonda's classroom and its impact on literacy learning.

By dragging and dropping the clips that are most appropriate to your study from the bank of clips across the bottom of the screen to the eight available windows of your study, and sequencing the chosen clips in the most appropriate order, you will complete the first step in creating your own study.

Study Builder – Step By Step

1. Decide on a focus
The possibilities are almost limitless. Whether you want to examine something as overarching as constructivism or as specific as the use of literature in the classroom, you'll find examples in these classrooms. For our purposes, we've decided to look at the physical environment of the classroom.

2. Select clips that illustrate your focus
You'll see the bank of 24 usable clips at the bottom of the window. The clips are numbered, and they are pulled from all four of the study sections on the CD. Select up to eight video clips that best illustrate the issues raised in your study focus.

In the case of our example study, clips 7, 8, 11 from Ms. Blake's classroom, and clip 20 from Ms. Turner's fourth grade classroom clearly illustrate different centers. This speaks directly to our focus on the physical structure of the classroom. We can begin with these clips, and possibly choose a handful of others to examine the whole group areas (perhaps clip 1 from Ms. Clark's Kindergarten classroom and clip 19 from Ms. Sundin's second grade classroom), as well as small group tables (clips 4 and 5 from Ms. Clark's Kindergarten classroom illustrate this well).

3. Drag and drop the clips into the eight open slots
Once you've selected the clips you want to use, you'll want to put them into an order that best illustrates the points you're garnering from the footage to help in answering your question. To do so, simply click on the clip you'd like to add, drag it into the slot that you wish to use, and drop it there.

For the purposes of our example study, we'll put the clips in an order that first illustrates literacy centers, and then look at small group environments, and finally at whole group environments.

4. Save and Name the study
Once you've selected the clips for your study, the next step is to save and name the study. Click the "Save Study" button toward the top of the screen. A small

window will pop up, asking for a name for the study. Enter the name for your study and click the "Save" button. For our study, we've selected the name "Classroom Setup."

5. Move on to the Custom Studies step
Now that your study is saved, it's time to move on to the Custom Studies tool to customize—and add information to—your study. Click on the "Custom Studies" button in the menu on the left side of the screen. You'll see that the study you've just created is already loaded into your Custom Studies list. You can create any number of new studies in this same manner.

If you have questions about this module's functionality, click on the help button ("?"), then on "Using the study builder" listed in the menu of Help topics.

Customizing Your Study

You've found footage concerning one specific aspect of teaching, and you've grouped the clips in the most appropriate way to create a study. Now you'll add your own commentary to each clip, filling out the case and documenting your own understanding of the focus of your study.

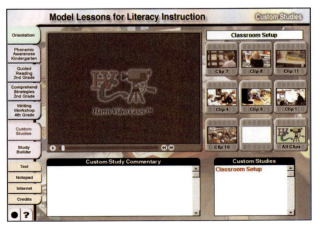

Custom Study – Step By Step

1. Open saved study
Click on the name of your saved study in the Custom Studies list to load it into the system. You'll see your study title at the top-right of the screen, and the clips you selected will fill in the bank below in the order you saved them. We've opened our "Classroom Setup" study.

2. Add your own commentary to each clip

When you click the mouse on one of the clips in the bank on the right, it will load the clip into the large video window. You will notice that a cursor appears and in the "Custom Study Commentary" field at the bottom of the screen. The video will begin playing automatically, and you can begin adding your thoughts or other supporting ideas to the commentary field. This is your opportunity to explain why this particular video clip is relevant to your focus. From our study, we've loaded clip 7, and will comment on Ms. Blake's use of centers to structure her classroom environment.

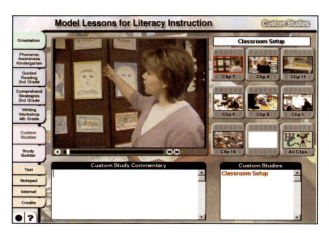

3. Add comments of your own, or pull comments from Notepad or the text button

The textual data that you use to make your case may consist of your own commentary, but you may also want to include pertinent information from the text already on the Virtual Classroom CD ROM, notes you've taken on the Notepad module, or material found on the Internet.

To access all the commentaries on the CD, click the Text Button to bring up the menu-driven text archive. Each of the CD's four lessons is listed in the menu, and each title is a hot link to that specific lesson's text. When you find the appropriate comments, simply highlight the section, use the edit button to copy the selection, and paste it into the commentary field on your custom study.

For our study, we've listed briefly how Mrs. Blake's "tour" of the study centers in her classroom helped to show how she teaches reading effectively in many different ways, and also how the organization of her centers is effective forgetting the best use out of them.

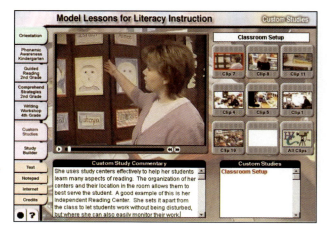

Besides utilizing the existing research for your study, you can, of course, type in your own thoughts or revisit your Notepad excerpts. You can also launch a search on the Internet with the CD's Internet button. From there you can either check out the literacy related links included in the module, or do your own search online.

4. *When you've added all your elements, save your study to your own hard drive or disk.*
Each custom study you create is saved by the template in the file that was created when the program was first opened. When you started, you had control over the name of this file and its location on the computer's hard disk. This means that these commentary files can be copied to floppy or Zip disks, or they can be uploaded to email or bulletin board contexts for sharing with other pre-service students or teacher educators. This capacity also means commentary files can be transferred from computer to computer if users are not always using the same computer for this CD-ROM work.

This "start-up" file houses all of your Custom Studies and their information, so make sure that you load that same file each time you start the CD. All of your Custom Study information will reload as well. Don't be alarmed that as you add commentary to a study there is no "Save" button to be found. Once you've added to the Commentary field, the study is automatically written to your master file.

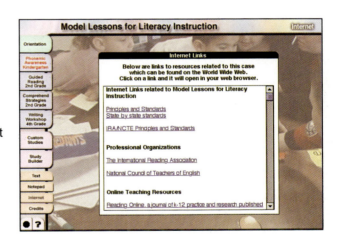

The Custom Studies tutorial found on the Help ("?") screen provides a helpful reminder, should you need any assistance while creating your study.